R.I.P. Emma Lou Briggs

a play in one act

by Dot Hatfield

R.I.P. Emma Lou Briggs, a play in one act by Dot Hatfield, directed by Lana Hallmark, was presented at Performing Arts Center on the Square in Searcy, Arkansas, July 15, 2011, with the following cast of characters:

Diane   Carolyn McNamee

Nikki   Madison Kuebler

Karen   Shelly White

JoEllen   Suzanne Guymon

Hal   J.R. Thomas

Suggested music:

Fill the World With Love
Music and Lyrics: Leslie Bricusse

Tapestry
Music and Lyrics: Carole King

R.I.P. Emma Lou Briggs

CAST:

DIANE	the oldest of Emma Lou's three daughters
NIKKI	DIANE'S daughter
KAREN	Emma Lou's second daughter
HAL	KAREN'S husband
JOELLEN	youngest of the three sisters

SETTING:

A small town in middle Tennessee. The action takes place in Emma Lou's living room, decorated in a style that could best be described as eclectic. A seventies-era couch and chair, bentwood rocker, antique china cabinet, console TV with rabbit ears, and a bookcase full of books. Along the wall stage left, is a portable stereo from the eighties and a stack of records. In the corner stage right, a small computer sits on a formica-top table. A door stage left leads to Emma Lou's bedroom. Center stage right is a door leading outside to the front porch.

TIME:

June, 2001, the day after Emma Lou Briggs' funeral. The song "Fill the World With Love" is heard in the background. *"Did I fill the world with love my whole life through…"*

> *(Lights up on empty stage. A key rattles in the lock and DIANE and NIKKI enter from outside.)*

NIKKI:

What's that smell?

DIANE:

It's just a little muggy in here. Turn on the air conditioner. Flip on the ceiling fan. Open the window.

NIKKI:

Which of those things do you want me to do?

DIANE:

All three.

NIKKI:

Why did Gram always keep the house so stuffy?

> *(SHE flips on fan and adjusts air conditioner. DIANE moves around the room 'straightening' things.)*

DIANE:

Oh, she didn't mean to. It's just that the last few years she was always cold. Blood gets thinner with age, you know.

NIKKI:

Yeah, I guess so. *(Sits on the couch.)* It was a nice service, Mom. What was that song the lady sang … from the old movie? I liked that.

DIANE:

"Fill the world with love…" Petula Clark sang it in *Goodbye Mr. Chips."* It was always one of Mom's favorites. I think it said a lot about her life, so I wanted to use it.

NIKKI:

She was a sweetie, all right. I should have come around more often, I guess, but …

DIANE:

She knew you were busy. She always wanted to know the latest news about you. That's why she bought that second-hand computer … so she could get email from her grandkids.

NIKKI:

Now you're making me feel guilty. I'm sorry I didn't write her more often ... or come see her. But I feel kinda creepy around old people. I don't know what to say ...

DIANE:

I hope you outgrow that sometime in the next thirty or forty years.

NIKKI:

Touché. Enough of that. What happened to all of Papa's stuff when he died?

DIANE:

Gosh, that was twenty years ago. Mama eventually gave his clothes to Goodwill. Kept his wedding suit, I think. It's probably still hanging in one of the upstairs closets. She drove the car till it fell apart. A couple of years ago she gave each of us something sentimental. We drew straws for wedding band, Kiwanis pin, Masonic ring – things like that. Who knows? When we look around, we might find more things of his she couldn't bear to part with.

NIKKI:

Twenty years ago. I guess Gram was pretty young to be a widow.

DIANE:

She was. We weren't sure how she would manage. My daddy was head of the household. Not mean or anything, but he made all the decisions. She went along with everything he wanted. That's the way it was back then. If she ever complained, I never heard of it. We wondered what would happen when a decision needed to be made and Daddy wasn't here to make it.

NIKKI:

So what happened?

DIANE:

She surprised us all. They had gotten married Mama's senior year in college. Then when JoEllen was old enough to start school, Mama asked Daddy about getting her teaching certificate. He said it was okay by him, so she did. She was just made for teaching. She loved it. And kids loved her.

NIKKI:

She asked his permission? What if he had said no?

DIANE:

If Daddy hadn't wanted her to work, she would have stayed a housewife.

(DIANE has pulled an old high school yearbook from the bookcase and shows it to NIKKI.)

NIKKI:
Look at that girl's hair! *(Laughing)*

DIANE:
Kinda flat on top, huh?

NIKKI:
Yeah, but the boys made up for it. What is that hairdo called?

DIANE:
That is a pompadour.

NIKKI:
Held in place with a quart of grease. (SHE flips a few pages) So when Papa died, she had the teaching job to fall back on.

DIANE:
Yes, but like I said she surprised us by deciding to go back to school and get her Masters. Hadn't set foot on a college campus for 30 years but she set her head to do it and she did.

NIKKI:

(*Smiling*) Without Papa saying it was okay?

DIANE:

I wondered at the time what he would have thought of it. Wonder if he'd have given permission if he were alive.

NIKKI:

Or if it was something she always wanted to do and couldn't.

DIANE:

Right. Then when the old car finally died, Mama was faced with having to buy another. Daddy had always bought the cars. He's just drive it home – usually surprising Mama with it.

NIKKI:

She never helped pick it out?

DIANE:

Nope. And she had no idea about the bargaining and trading. How the car dealers ask one price and you're supposed to haggle with them to get the price down. Daddy loved that sort of thing, rose to the challenge. Mama didn't have a clue.

NIKKI:

So what did she do?

DIANE:

Like any good teacher, she did her homework. She looked up makes and models and prices. This was before the internet, remember. She collared a salesman on one of the lots and got a lot of information from him. Then she figured out how much she should pay and how much interest.

NIKKI:

So how could she know if she was getting a lemon?

DIANE:

Well, she knew she couldn't afford a new car and it's hard to determine when a used car is in good shape, so she went to the Hertz Used Car place in Nashville. They put a sticker on the car – no haggling. And all the history of the car is an open book. So she just picked one out, called her bank and made the deal. She drove that Taurus for ten years.

NIKKI:

That's a great story, Mom. Did Gram ever think about getting married again?

DIANE:

Not that I know of. Mr. Billingsley took her out to
dinner a few times but I think they were just friends.

NIKKI:

That's something I would like to know more about. You
know, Mom, I wonder how often that will happen.

DIANE:

What?

NIKKI:

That something will come to mind I wish I had asked
Gram about. She was so smart and had a wonderful
memory. I loved her stories when I was little and now
when I think of the tales she told, I want to ask more
questions, clarify points, get names. Now it's too late.

*(NIKKI rises and circles the room, peering in the
china cabinet, looking at the pictures, books, etc.)*

When do the rest of them get here?

DIANE:

Anytime now, I guess. Karen and Hal are picking up
JoEllen.

NIKKI:

Uncle Hal's coming?

DIANE:

Don't start.

NIKKI:

What about the twins?

DIANE:

They left this morning for cheerleading camp. A day late because of the funeral. George took them down. That's why JoEllen is coming with Karen and Hal.

(NIKKI scans the record collection near the stereo.)

NIKKI:

Look at these old LPs. Did Gram play them anymore?

DIANE:

I'm not sure the stereo even works.

NIKKI:

Here's that movie album – *"Goodbye Mr. Chips – 1960."* ... a forty-year-old record.

(SHE continues to flip through album covers.)

Oh, my gosh. Here's Carole King's *Tapestry* album. That's a classic. Mom! On the back Gram wrote "from Di, Christmas 1972." You gave this to her! Did Gram like Carole King?

DIANE:
I guess so. Actually, those were all my favorite songs. I bought that for her when I was in college. I nearly wore it thin, I loved it so.

NIKKI:
Well, they say a thoughtful gift is something *you* like.

DIANE:
Doesn't seem so thoughtful, now. To tell the truth, it feels a little selfish. Like I didn't think of what she might want for Christmas. I did it for myself.

NIKKI:
Knowing Gram, she loved this. (SHE moves over to the bookcase.)

Wow! That's a bunch of books. Gram must have kept every one she ever read.

DIANE:

No, impossible. But probably every one that was a gift. She never threw away or recycled a gift. If it wasn't used up, like food or hand lotion, it's still here somewhere.

NIKKI:

Hey, look. You're right. *(Reading from book.)* "*Listen to the Warm,* poems by Rod McKuen."

DIANE:

Oh my gosh.

NIKKI:

It says, "from Karen, 1975. Mom, hope you love this as much as I do." (*SHE randomly reads aloud from the book, laughing.*) So, what do you think? Did Gram like this poetry?

DIANE:

(Laughing.) She probably preferred Helen Steiner Rice. But I imagine she loved the gift because Karen chose it. And it gave her an idea about what Karen liked.

> (*KAREN enters, followed by her husband, HAL, and her sister, JOELLEN. All three are dressed casually but it's clear that KAREN'S outfit came from an upscale shop. HAL wears shorts and a golf shirt.*)

KAREN:

Did I hear my name mentioned?

DIANE:

Hi. Nikki found an old book you gave Mom.

KAREN:

I wouldn't be surprised. She never threw anything away.

HAL:

Okay. Let's get started. We want to leave first thing tomorrow.

DIANE:

Well, this is something we need to take care of. It may take awhile and I don't want to rush through it.

HAL:

Listen, Di … (HE shrugs.) Okay, I think I'll pull the car into the yard under the shade tree.

(HE leaves)

DIANE:

Karen, I will not be rushed through taking care of Mother's things just because Hal is on a deadline. We sisters need to do this together and he can just butt out.

KAREN:
No need to get all huffy. Hal has a business to run. This trip is taking money out of his pocket, you know.

DIANE:
Karen, for God's sake, our mother just died. I'm grieving about that. I need time with my sisters to deal with our loss and decide what to do with all her things.

JOELLEN:
Please, can't we do this without you two fighting? We need to agree about what's going on.

KAREN:
Well, we're going to have an estate sale, aren't we? All these antiques ... that Depression Glass alone is worth a fortune.

JOELLEN:
But that belonged to Granny West, didn't it?

KAREN:
Jo, I've seen your house. You don't need any more knick-knacks collecting dust.

DIANE:

Okay. Wait. I know Mom wrote down some of her wishes. Maybe not an official will, but at least some guidelines so we can know what she wanted to happen.

JOELLEN:

That would help a lot...

DIANE:

Are you two agreeable to Nikki to take a look around Mom's room to see if she can find anything?

KAREN:

Sure, the quicker we get this settled the better.

DIANE:

Do you mind, Nikki? Just look through the desks and end tables, maybe the dresser and cedar chest. See if you can find a piece of paper that might give us an idea about what she wanted done.

NIKKI:

Sure.

> *(NIKKI goes into the bedroom as HAL comes in from outside.)*

HAL:
How are things coming along?

KAREN:
Nikki's looking for a will or something and we are about to discuss how to get rid of all the household items.

HAL:
An estate sale – right?

DIANE:
That's not been decided.

HAL:
Why not? It's the most sensible...

DIANE:
Not for all of us.

HAL:
Karen, I can't stay here forever. You said this wouldn't take long.

KAREN:
We have to talk through a few things first. We can do that while Nikki's looking.

(HAL pulls out his cell phone and engages in a conversation. HE eventually leaves during the following.)

DIANE:

Now, about a sale. We may need to have one eventually to clear out the last of it. But I think most of these things have sentimental value. Some of it I would like to keep, and I think Nikki would like to have a memento of her grandmother.

KAREN:

Nikki!

JOELLEN:

I think Jan and Joy would like something, too.

KAREN:

The grandchildren shouldn't even be considered in the division of things. That isn't fair to me. I don't have a child.

DIANE:

(Aside) That's debatable.

KAREN:

What was that?

JOELLEN:
Never mind. I know my girls will want a remembrance.
I'll share with them. If we each choose three items, I can
keep one and give one to each of my girls. Di will pick
three and give something to Nikki and you will have
three to do with as you please. Let's just don't fight!

KAREN:
You have to realize that everything you give your girls
cuts into my share – takes away from the profit of the
estate sale.

DIANE:
Fine by me. I don't care if we never make a cent from an
estate sale.

(NIKKI appears from the bedroom.)

NIKKI:
Did you know Gram kept a journal?

(The three women stare at her, make no response.)

NIKKI:

She did. She wrote her thoughts on current affairs, news about us, and reflections on things she read. Listen to this: "May 9, 1999. Today is Mother's Day, but no cards or calls. I know the girls are busy, but how do you forget Mother's Day? There are quite a few reminders around, after all." Then she wrote a memory about Granny West.

JOELLEN:

We all forgot Mother's Day? What year was that?

NIKKI:

1999.

JOELLEN:

I always sent something … I was probably late.

KAREN:

I don't go in for these holidays dreamed up by big business. I did things for her at other times during the year. I may have passed up Mother's Day occasionally because I don't believe in it.

DIANE:
Oh, give it a rest, Karen. I think that was the year I had been here just the week before. I guess I thought that was enough. I never thought how that might feel to her.

NIKKI:
I'd sure never get by with an excuse like that.

(DIANE scorches her with a look.)

KAREN:
Never mind all that. Nikki, if Mom kept a journal, that's the logical place to find a will.

NIKKI:
Oh … Oh … Listen to this: "Well, it's not going to happen. I thought George Billingsley was someone I could love, could enjoy growing old with. Have some companionship. But this is the end of that dream. It will never happen now. It's a little sad to think of going on alone, but there are worse things than being alone.'

JOELLEN:
What is that about?

DIANE:

You remember. She and Mr. Billingsley went out a few times.

JOELLEN:

Oh, yes. That friend of Daddy's ...

KAREN:

Really? You think they seriously talked about getting married or something?

JOELLEN:

And then didn't for some reason?

NIKKI:

Wonder what happened?

DIANE:

I don't suppose we'll ever know.

KAREN:

Maybe he was impotent. I've read a lot of articles about how seniors still enjoy sex.

> (*JOELLEN claps her hands over her ears. NIKKI laughs aloud. DIANE and JOELLEN speak simultaneously.*)

JOELLEN:
(hands over ears) La, la, la, la, la,la

DIANE:
Karen! For Pete's sake!

KAREN:
What?

DIANE:
Well, for one thing, when Mama and Mr. Billingsley were going out she wasn't much older than I am, thank you very much.

JOELLEN:
And I don't want to talk about this!

DIANE:
Nikki, keep looking. And stop reading unless it has to do with what we're looking for. Also, I think she had one of those fire-proof boxes. It's blue … about the size of a tackle box.

(NIKKI leaves as HAL enters from the front porch.)

HAL:
Are we making any progress at all? Karen, need I remind you we have a flight tomorrow morning?

DIANE:

Hal, why don't you go ahead and go on back. Karen can stay here with us for a few days and help get this all settled.

HAL:

Karen has responsibilities, too. The Junior League is having a major fundraiser at Christmas and she is on the planning committee.

DIANE:

Junior League? Are you kidding me? Isn't that for twenty-something socialites? And Karen has to help them plan an event that's still six months away?

HAL:

As a Past President, Karen is on the advisory committee and still an active part of the organization. She connects with women whose husbands are business associates of mine. Her work with charity functions helps me tremendously.

DIANE:

It seems to me that this is important, too. Karen needs…

KAREN:

Will you two PLEASE stop talking about me as though I were on Mars? I'm right here in the same room with you and capable of speaking for myself.

JOELLEN:

Come on ... Karen ... Diane ... please don't argue. Can't we just agree to discuss this peaceably? Where were we? Oh yes ... everyone choose three things.

KAREN:

And the rest goes to an estate sale?

DIANE:

We have to go through it first.

KAREN:

There are companies that do that.

JOELLEN:

I'm with Di on this one. I hate to think of strangers pawing through Mom's stuff.

KAREN:

Oh, for Pete's sake.

HAL:

Karen's right. I think...

DIANE:

Hal, I don't give a flip what you think. Just stay out of this. I don't know why you came along on this trip but I will not have you rush me. This is not your mother. When your mother dies you can ransack her house any way you want to. But right now, you can get out of my mother's house and don't come back.

HAL:

I have a right to be here...

DIANE:

No, you don't. Not if I don't want you here. Get out!

HAL:

Karen...?

DIANE:

Get out!

KAREN:

Di...

DIANE:

Shut up. You can get out, too. If you don't want to be a part of this, go on home and suck up to your husband's friends.

JOELLEN:
(Near tears) Please... *please.* Diane ... Karen ... we're sisters. We're all we have now. Don't do this...

HAL:
All right. I can tell when I'm not welcome. Karen, I'm going back to the hotel. Do you want to come?

> *(KAREN doesn't answer and no one speaks for full beat.)*

JOELLEN:
If you want to stay, Karen, George will come pick us up when he gets back from camp, I'm sure. I'll just need to call...

KAREN:
Does Di want me to stay?

JOELLEN:
Do you, Diane?

DIANE:
Sure. *(Grudgingly)* And Nikki and I can drive you where you need to go.

KAREN:
Okay. Hal, you go on. I'll be along later.

(HAL throws up his hands and stomps out of the house. The women sit and stare at the floor for a few moments. The tension is thick enough to slice.)

JOELLEN:

Now. Isn't this nice? It's good for the three of us to be together. It doesn't happen very often. We won't have Mom's house to gather in from now on. We'll have to plan another place and be sure to make time for each other. We have to stick together. We're the oldest generation now.

KAREN:

Morbid thought.

DIANE:

She's right, though. We shouldn't fight. I'm sorry I blew my stack. I'm really sad about losing Mom. I can't be as matter-of-fact as you are about it. Getting rid of her things will be like losing her all over again. Keeping something that belonged to her will be like having a part of her for awhile longer.

KAREN:

Okay. I can deal with that.

JOELLEN:

We all feel differently about this, I guess, but there's no reason we can't reach an agreement that we'll all be okay with.

(*NIKKI comes in quickly.*)

NIKKI:

I think I found it!

(*The three women gather around, looking over NIKKI'S shoulder at the paper she holds.*)

KAREN:

Are you sure?

NIKKI:

I think so. The outside of the envelope says "To My Children." It's dated back in 2000 and she says it's her last wishes.

JOELLEN:

I think we need to sit down and let Nikki read this. Mom obviously thought things through and wrote some notes for us to go by.

DIANE:

Good idea, Jo. Let's hear what Mom had to say.

NIKKI:

"To Diane, Karen and JoEllen: First of all, don't worry about me. I'm safe in the arms of Jesus. Today is the first day of a new century, a day I never thought I would live to see. I didn't go to a lawyer and spend the money on a will because I know that writing it down this way is legal and binding if I say I want it to be. Also, I trust you girls to do what I want, although I know Diane can be bossy, Karen cares a lot about money and JoEllen will make any compromise to keep the peace." *(NIKKI looks at her mother and her aunts.)* I think Gram had you three pegged.

DIANE:

Just go on, please.

NIKKI:

"Last year, I put all my interests in joint ownership with you girls. Diane has the equity in the house and furniture, Karen is beneficiary on my insurance policies and JoEllen, my teacher retirement IRA. At the time this was done, these were fairly equal amounts. I hope they still are."

(Pause)

NIKKI:

"So, you girls have what you have. Everything else goes to my granddaughters. First, I want Diane, Karen, JoEllen and Nikki to choose one item of sentiment from either the china cabinet or my jewelry case. After that is done, the china cabinet, which belonged to my mother, and all its contents, I leave to my granddaughter, Joy. My jewelry case, which my father bought for my mother at the 1932 World's Fair, and all its contents, I leave to my granddaughter, Jan. These things should be kept for them by their parents until they are of legal age. At that time, should Joy or Jan decide to sell part of their inheritance, family members should be given the first opportunity to buy.

"To Nikki, because she is a budding writer, I leave my journals and my books. I hope my story will inspire some stories of your own. And, lest you think this is a less valuable gift than what your cousins received, you should browse through the bookcase. You will find a first edition of *The Great Gatsby* and a signed copy of *To Kill a Mockingbird.*"

> (NIKKI stops reading, overcome with emotion. SHE clears her throat.)

I can't believe it. Her journals …

JOELLEN:

She was so proud of your writing. Always bragging on you.

KAREN:

Is that all she said?

NIKKI:

(Continues to read) "You three girls brought great joy into my life and I thanked God for you every morning in my prayers. The life I had was happy and complete. I hope one day you can say the same." She signed it, "Emma Lou Briggs, January 1, 2000."

> *(SHE slowly looks around the room at each of the women.)*

She added a p.s. "My cedar chest and its contents belong to Karen, to share with her sisters however she chooses."

> *(Silence – each one sits with her own thoughts.)*

KAREN:

So. That's it. Someone got a phone? I'll call Hal to come back and get me.

JOELLEN:
Oh, don't leave yet, Karen. Stay awhile.

DIANE:
That's a good idea. I'll make some tea…

NIKKI:
Yeah, Aunt Karen. You really need to check out that cedar chest. It's full of baby books and little toys and picture albums. All three of you should look through that stuff. Which one of you won a spelling bee ribbon?

KAREN:
That would be me. She kept that? Really?

NIKKI:
Really. No kidding, you should look.

DIANE:
We could do it together …

> (DIANE stands and holds out her hand to KAREN, who takes it as they exit stage left into Emma Lou's room. JOELLEN follows. NIKKI is left alone. SHE speaks to their retreating backs.)

NIKKI:

Okay, you all go look ... I'll wait out here ... I'll just be sitting in the porch swing.

> *(SHE walks to the stereo and turns it on. The music begins as she stops at the door, turns and looks back into the room.)*

NIKKI:

Thanks, Gram. You did good. Now rest in peace.

> *(The outside door closes softly behind NIKKI as we hear the voice of Carole King. "My life has been a tapestry of rich and royal hue...")*

FADE TO DARK

About the Author

Dot Hatfield is a mom and grandma who began writing seriously after retiring from The Rape and Sexual Abuse Center in Nashville, Tennessee in 2000. Her short stories and articles have appeared in several state and regional newspapers and magazines.

A collection of award-winning short stories appeared in 2006 under the title *Every Day a New Day and other short stories*. Dot has also written two novels, *The Last to Know* and *To Find a Home*.

Dot lives in Beebe, Arkansas where she is active in church and community activities, including appearing on stage at Center On The Square dinner theater in Searcy from time to time. She is past president of White County Creative Writers and a member of Central Arkansas Writers and Ozark Writers League. Visit her website and blog at dothatfield.com.

www.ingramcontent.com/pod-product-compliance
Lightning Source LLC
Chambersburg PA
CBHW021121020426
42331CB00004B/576